A carved plane, 12 inches (300 mm) long, made of boxwood and hornbeam. Although it is elaborately decorated, it was intended for use and its sole has been plated with copper to resist wear.

WOODWORKING TOOLS

Philip Walker

Shire Publications Ltd

CONTENTS

Set in 9 on 9 point English roman and printed in Great Britain by C. I. Thomas & Sons (Haverfordwest) Ltd, Press Buildings, Merlins Bridge, Haverfordwest.

Photographs by John Melville

COVER: *The tools shown are a massive carpenter's hewing axe, weighing 6½ lb (2.9 kg) (German, sixteenth or seventeenth century), a carved beech smoothing plane (Dutch, 1795), and a brass-framed ebony brace (English, nineteenth century). (Photograph by Studio 10, London).*

A selection of chisels, scrapers, gouges, augers and other edge tools from the 1889 'Illustrated Trade List of Prices of Sheffield Goods'.

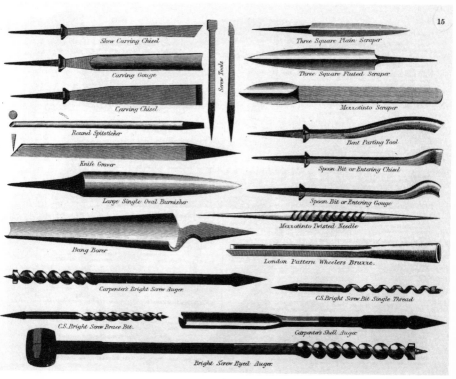

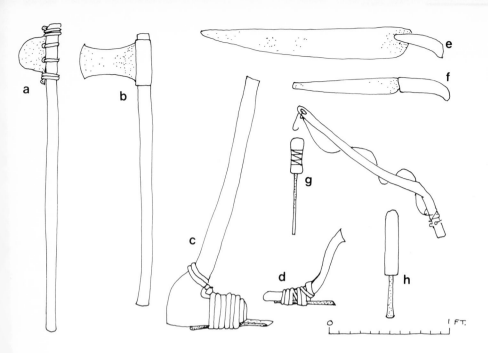

Ancient Egyptian tools. (a) An axe which is simply a semicircular plate thickened along its straight edge, which rests against the haft and is held there by hide strips passing through holes and over lugs. (b) An axe of later form but basically the same idea. Although it appears to have a socket this was probably only a tube of leather or gut which was passed over the blade and then dried and shrunk on to the haft. (c) Two-handed adze. (d) Single-handed adze. (e, f) Two saws, both capable of cutting on the pull stroke only. (g) A bow-drill and its bow. (h) A chisel.

HISTORICAL DEVELOPMENT

The ancient Egyptians have left us a vivid picture of woodworking in their time. Not only paintings and engravings on flat surfaces but full three-dimensional models show all aspects of their everyday life and work from five thousand years ago. The exceptionally dry climate of Egypt has preserved these models, together with quantities of the tools themselves, furniture and other artifacts which were put into tombs in the belief that their owners would need them in their life after death. Thus, although man has been working wood with tools of a sort for about half a million years, it is to the Egyptians that we owe our earliest record of a distinct woodworking trade with its own specialised tool kit.

The ancient Egyptians had many of the basic woodworking tools: axes for felling trees and for shaping them roughly into balks; saws for ripping timber along the grain and also for cross-cutting it to the desired length; adzes for shaping and for smoothing surfaces; chisels for carving and for chopping out mortises; bow-drills for boring small holes.

The principal technical limitations of the Egyptians were the quality of the metal available to them and the methods used to fix tools to their handles. The metal used at first was copper, which could not be hardened to hold a good edge until, sometime in the second millennium BC, the advantage of adding tin to the copper, thus making bronze, became known. For fixing axe and adze heads to their hafts the Egyptians relied on binding with thongs of hide or sinew. The much more effective method of wedging the haft into an eye or socket formed in the axe head was used quite early, in parts of Asia and then in Crete, but does not seem to have been thought of in Egypt until it was

Egyptian tools in use. Illustrations taken from tombs dating between about 2400 and 1400 BC. The drilling scene (bottom right) is particularly interesting as it shows the assistant applying pressure on to some sort of bearing at the top of the drill.

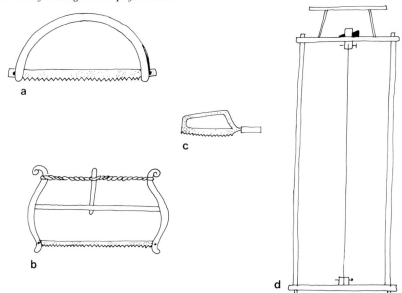

a

c

b

d

Roman saws. (a) A true 'bow' saw, where the tension on the blade is applied by a stick bent into a semicircle — the same principle as the tubular steel bow of a modern Swedish log saw. (b) A framed saw with the tension provided by a twisted cord, as in English turning saws of the present day. (c) A small saw forged in a single piece of metal and looking remarkably like a modern hacksaw. Tension on the blade would have had to be maintained by hammering the top bar. (d) A two-man framed saw, indistinguishable from saws used for ripping trees into boards in France until very recently. Contemporary illustrations do not show clearly the method of applying tension to the blade, so the wedge is conjectural.

imported by the Greeks or Romans.

By the time Rome was at the height of its power considerable advances had been made. Iron was plentiful and, even though the Romans did not know how to make steel in the modern sense, they managed to harden the cutting edges of their tools adequately for the purpose. Even more important were the improvements in methods of attaching tools to their handles. Saw blades, which the Egyptians had had to operate with a pull stroke only, because the blades would buckle up if pushed, were now held under tension in a frame and could safely be pushed or pulled. Axe heads had a hole, or 'eye', into which the haft could be wedged. Moreover, that most characteristic tool of the modern woodworker, the plane, had been introduced. It was probably a Greek who invented the tool but no example of an ancient Greek plane has survived whereas there are a number of Roman ones, of quite sophisticated design, to produce both flat and shaped ('moulded') surfaces.

Roman planes look remarkably modern and, indeed, so many of the basic tools had by then been developed into almost their final form that if a Roman carpenter and a modern carpenter were magically transported into each other's workshops they would find the tools sufficiently familiar to finish the job in hand.

The Roman craftsman's main handicap was his lack of a tool which would bore a hole of reasonable size, say ½ inch (13 mm) or over, by continuous rotation. Like the Egyptians, the Romans used the bow-drill for small holes and they had, in addition, augers to which sufficient force could be applied to bore large holes. But turning an auger is a tedious, hand-over-hand task and it is surprising that the Romans did not think of the brace-and-bit or, indeed, the idea of the crank in any form at all.

A brace, or 'bitstock' as it is often called when it has a bit permanently fixed in place, is an invaluable tool, not only for making holes, up to about 2 inches (50 mm) in diameter, but also as the quickest way of removing waste wood, for example when preparing a mortise. Nobody knows when or by whom it was invented. The earliest known illustrations of braces date from the beginning of the fifteenth century. However the tools shown appear to be fully evolved — they do not look as though a new idea is just being tried out — so it seems that the crank principle must have been used for boring in the fourteenth century at the latest. No brace appears among the tools being used by the shipbuilders in the Bayeux Tapestry (executed around 1090) but a type of auger with a distinct improvement is clearly shown. This is the breast-auger, that is to say an auger with a loose revolving head which enables the user to keep the pressure on it with his chest while his hands concentrate on the turning effort.

In most cases early braces were made entirely of wood, apart from the metal bit which was fixed into them. However one, depicted on a seal in 1407, is metal with a so-called 'cage-head', namely a flat head, revolving on a central point bearing and kept in place by a cage of two or more arms — a similar arrangement to the

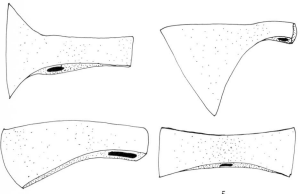

Roman axeheads found at Pompeii, where they had lain since AD 79. Just like modern axes, they have eyes into which the hafts would be wedged.

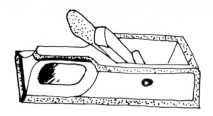

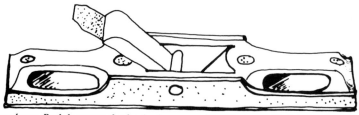

Two Roman planes. Both have metal soles for long wear. Rigidity is provided, in the long one, by the metal sides and, in the other, by the metal plate bent over the front and top.

mounting used in the eighteenth century for some round table tops.

Roman saws were mostly framed although there is evidence that there were some small ones with open blades designed to cut on the push stroke — just as modern handsaws do. Medieval woodworkers continued to use the framed types but they also introduced a large push saw with a blade 3 feet or more (1 metre) in length. These saws had teeth sharply raked towards the front, a long, straight wooden handle and something like a sword guard to save the hand from slipping on to the teeth if the saw suddenly jammed in the middle of a stroke. This type of saw was certainly in use by the beginning of the fifteenth century and continued into the seventeenth century.

It could be said that since the end of the middle ages no really new hand tools have been introduced, although it is always possible to argue about whether a tool is new or merely the development of an old idea. The most obvious improvements in the last few hundred years have been developments and new applications of the screw — the screw being a very old idea, as

is shown by the screw-operated instruments discovered at Pompeii, where they had been buried in the lava since AD 79. As a way of joining pieces of wood together screws were coming into general use in the mid eighteenth century but it was not until the introduction of effective machinery for mass-producing them, a hundred years later, that they became cheap and plentiful. From then on there was increasingly wide application of the screw principle to all sorts of vices, cramps and other holding devices, as well as to the adjustment and mechanism of tools, including the now necessary screwdrivers themselves! Thus, for example, from the 1860s there were braces with screw chucks to hold any one of a variety of bits; gauges and compasses, the setting of which could be altered or locked by screw; planes with screw adjustments to their cutters; and drills or screwdrivers fitted with an Archimedean screw so that they could be worked with a pumping action. About the same time gear wheels were used in hand drills to alter the direction of drive and, sometimes, to increase the speed of rotation.

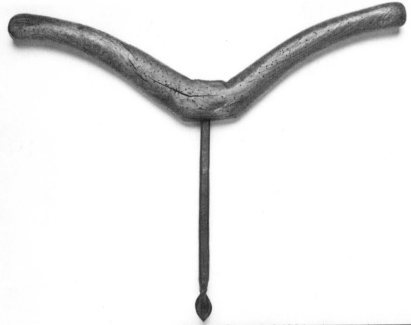

ABOVE: *An auger of the type used in the middle ages.*

RIGHT: *An auger in use, in a painting of about 1640.*

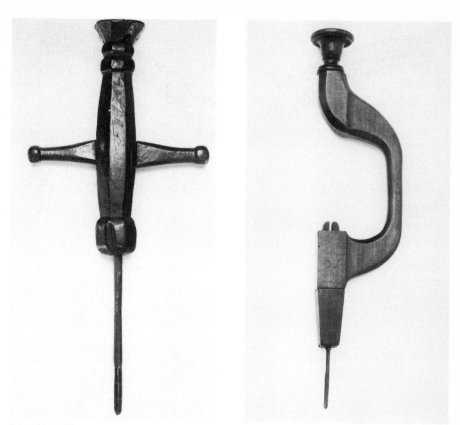

ABOVE LEFT: *A breast auger with a revolving head which enables the user to apply pressure with his chest.*
ABOVE RIGHT: *A wooden brace similar to ones which appear in fifteenth-century pictures.*

An iron brace with a centre-point bearing in the head, which is held on by a 'cage'.

ABOVE: *A type of brace (patented 1859), making use of the screw. Here the frame of the tool is split and the screw pinches it on to the bit.*

BELOW: *A brace with a screw in its chuck to hold interchangeable bits.*

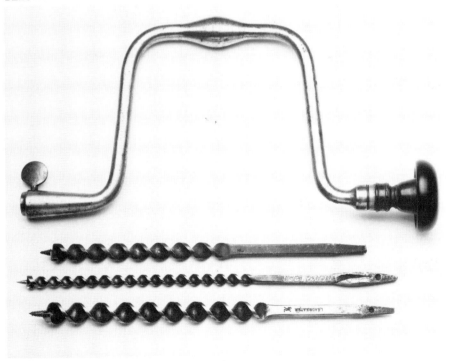

BAILEY'S PATENT WOOD PLANES.

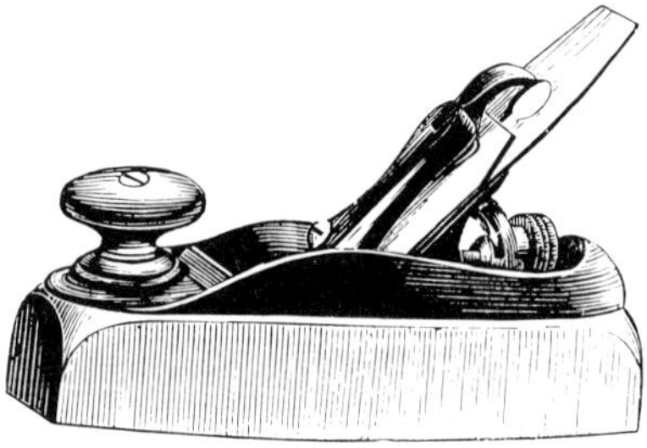

No.							Each.
21.	Smooth Plane	7 inches in length,	1¾ inch Cutter,	.	.	.	$3.00
22.	" "	8 " "	1¾ " "	.	.	.	3.00
23.	" "	9 " "	1¾ " "	.	.	.	3.00
24.	" "	8 " "	2 " "	.	.	.	3.00
25.	Block "	9½ " "	1¾ " "	.	.	.	3.00

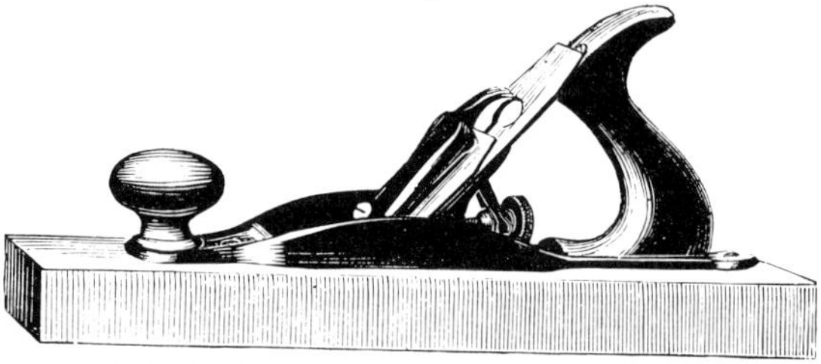

26.	Jack Plane,	15 inches in length,	2 inch Cutter,	4.00
27.	" "	15 " "	2⅛ " "	4.00
28.	Fore "	18 " "	2⅜ " "	4.50
29.	" "	20 " "	2⅜ " "	4.50
30.	Jointer "	22 " "	2⅜ " "	4.75
31.	" "	24 " "	2⅜ " "	4.75
32.	" "	26 " "	2⅝ " "	5.50
33.	" "	28 " "	2⅝ " "	5.50
34.	" "	30 " "	2⅝ " "	5.75

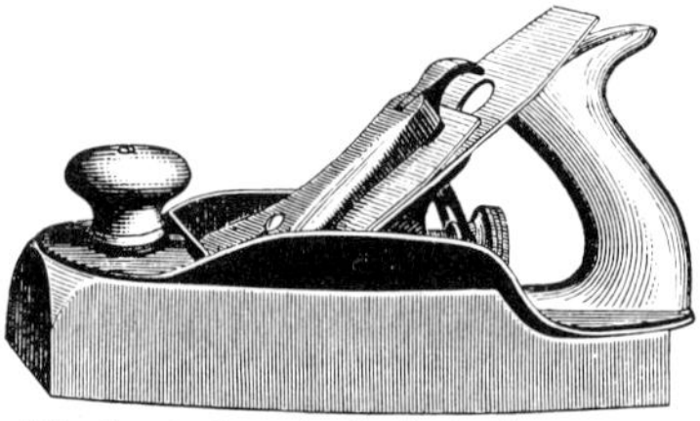

35.	Handle Smooth,	9 inches in length,	2 inch Cutter,	4.00
36.	" "	10 " "	2⅜ " "	4.50
37.	Jenny "	13 " "	2⅝ " "	4.50

[See recommendations on next page.]

Three planes with screw adjustment for their cutters. Taken from the 1870 catalogue of the American Stanley Rule and Level Company (Ken Roberts Publishing Co. reprint).

A variety of nineteenth-century drills which make use of various types of screw or gearing.

11

A group of axes, showing some of the variations possible on a basically simple idea. The axe second from the right is a broad axe of the so-called goose-wing type, common in the sixteenth century. It was intended for hewing wood but its point may have been found handy as a weapon on occasion.

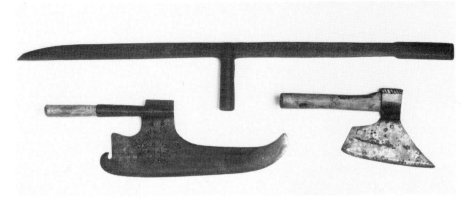

Below a carpenter's twybill are two axes used for hewing tree trunks into square balks in the days before sawmills had reached their present state of efficiency — or before machinery made it relatively easy to move trees from the forest to the sawmill.

VARIATIONS ON THE BASIC FORMS

We have dealt, very briefly and with many simplifications, with the basic woodworking tools. We will now look at the variety which these basic types have exhibited at different times and places. First it should be pointed out that most workmen, throughout most of history, made the wooden parts of their own tools, and that the metal parts were made locally by the nearest blacksmith. Therefore, although workmen in any culture tend to stick conservatively to the accepted patterns, absolute standardisation was not to be expected until a toolmaking industry arose and distributed its products throughout the country.

The axe is the fundamental woodworking tool. Most people nowadays probably think of axes simply as tools for cutting trees down and chopping them up for firewood, without realising that they were also used for all sorts of different shaping purposes: from squaring a tree trunk into a beam to cutting out mortises; from listing (i.e. bevelling and tapering) the staves for a cask to putting the point on trenails (i.e. tree-nails, the wooden pins or dowels formerly used so much in carpentry and shipbuilding). Axes used for shaping are usually sharpened with a bevel on one side only, like chisels, and are therefore known as side axes. Like chisels

also, they can be used with a paring or slicing movement and indeed it is hard to decide whether some tools, such as the carpenter's twybill or the thrust-axe (two tools which have been used until quite recently in some continental European countries), should be classified with axes or with chisels. Because of their weight, shaping axes do not have to be swung hard to make an effective cut. A short, light chop is usually sufficient and, unlike the chisel and mallet which they can replace, they leave the left hand free to hold the work. They are therefore easier and safer to use whenever it is not possible to hold the work firmly in a bench vice. The long twybill and the thrust-axe are also handier when the job — perhaps a beam to be jointed — is lying on the ground and cannot be raised to bench height.

The adze is closely related to the axe. It, too, is primarily a shaping tool but it was also used for smoothing and, in the hands of a skilled operator, can produce a surface to rival that from a plane. Gouge or bowl adzes existed in a variety of shapes and sizes. In addition to their use by some coopers for cleaning up the inside of casks, they were used to hollow out all manner of everyday objects such as rain gutters, pig troughs, milkmaids' yokes and chair seats.

13

An adze held to its handle by a method which has been in use for about 2500 years and is still used in southern European countries. The iron loop, which replaced the even earlier leather thongs, has the advantage that it can easily be slipped off and the tool taken apart so that the blade can be held against a grindstone.

LEFT: *An adze with a gouge-shaped blade, useful for all sorts of hollowing-out jobs. This particular one is believed to have been used mainly for making conduits, or gutters, out of straight pine poles, which are first split down the centre.*

BELOW: *Two saws for cutting grooves, for example to house stair treads or bookcase shelves.*

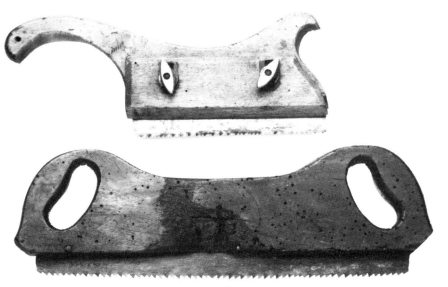

ABOVE LEFT: *Large framed saw similar to those used as an alternative to the open pitsaw. This particular example, which has a very thin blade in a narrow, decorative frame, was used for cutting balks of fine timber into veneers.*

ABOVE RIGHT: *Pitsaw, 8 feet (2.4m) long. This type of open-bladed saw, used to rip trees laid lengthwise over a pit into boards, was probably invented in England in the eighteenth century. Before that time framed saws seem to have been used, and the tree was propped up on a trestle so that the lower sawyer could work without need for a pit, a method still practised in many parts of the world.*

*A carpenter's twybill (a), a hurdle-maker's twybill (b), thrust-axes (c and d) and a shipwright's slice (e),
together with other chisels. One of the thrust-axes is fitted with a handle, but this may be a mistaken
reconstruction as the general opinion is that neither these tools nor the long carpenter's twybill were
used with handles. Thrust-axes and twybills are still used in some continental European countries.*

17

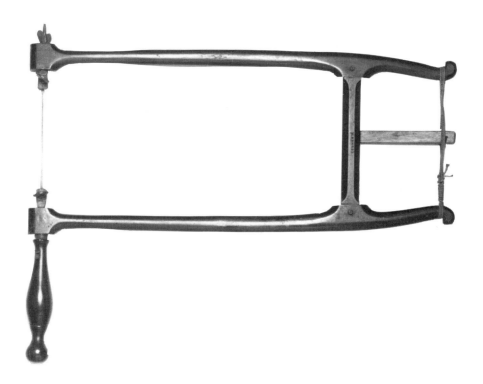

ABOVE: *A beautifully proportioned fret saw, made of mahogany.*

BELOW: *A saw designed for cutting off projecting dowel ends flush with the surface of the work.*

Saws have ranged in size from pitsaws, 8 feet or more (2.4 metres) long, for ripping trees along their length to make boards, down to tiny piercing and turning saws for the most delicate fretted work.

Planes exhibit the greatest variety of all. On the one hand planes have been devised to produce semi-automatically, i.e. by the simple process of pushing them forward, any object or shape which can be viewed as a single linear surface. Thus, in addition to an infinite range of planes for working decorative mouldings, there have been planes for making parallel packing strips for printers, planes for tapering fishing rods, planes for producing lighting spills, and even planes to put the notches in wedges for more planes! On the other hand there are planes which are func-tionally simple but which are exceptionally fine examples of the planemaker's art, or which have been embellished by their owners. These special tools seem to have been made in every age, from Roman times to the present. Many were unique items, conceived and created in the leisure hours of their owners, but some were made, as a regular line, at those periods when a sort of artisan aristocracy could afford something precious and ap-propriate to their status.

Different countries have also had their different tool shapes, just as they have had their characteristic clothing, although tools, like clothes, are now rapidly becoming standardised throughout the world.

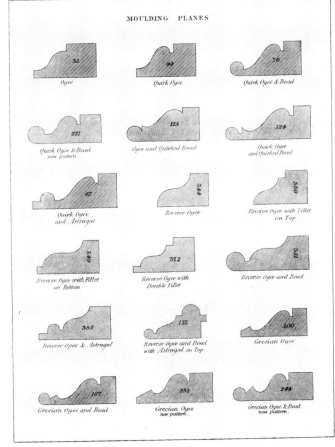

Some of the 546 different moulding-plane profiles offered by one tool manufacturer in 1899. (From the 1899 catalogue of Alex Mathieson & Sons, reprinted by Ken Roberts Publishing Co.)

ABOVE: *A sixteenth-century iron plane, one of a large series of similarly decorated tools probably made for royal or aristocratic amateurs.*

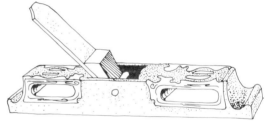

ABOVE: *A Roman plane of specially fine and decorative construction. It was found at Cologne and can now be seen in the Rhineland Museum in Bonn. It is in an astonishingly good state of preservation, although the wooden parts have been reconstructed in this illustration.*

BELOW: *A Dutch panel-fielding plane dated 1790. Planes of this design, of which large numbers have survived, were evidently made as a regular line by several professional planemakers.*

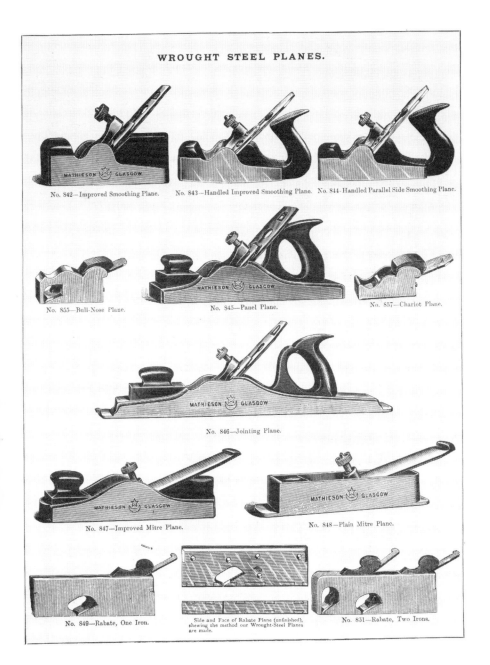

WROUGHT STEEL PLANES.

No. 842—Improved Smoothing Plane.   No. 843—Handled Improved Smoothing Plane.   No. 844-Handled Parallel Side Smoothing Plane.

No. 855—Bull-Nose Plane.   No. 845—Panel Plane.   No. 857—Chariot Plane.

No. 846—Jointing Plane.

No. 847—Improved Mitre Plane.   No. 848—Plain Mitre Plane.

No. 849—Rabate, One Iron.   Side and Face of Rabate Plane (unfinished), shewing the method our Wrought-Steel Planes are made.   No. 851—Rabate, Two Irons.

A selection of the steel planes available from Alex Mathieson & Sons in 1899 (Ken Roberts Publishing Co. catalogue reprint) with an illustration showing how these planes were made from steel plates dovetail-jointed together.

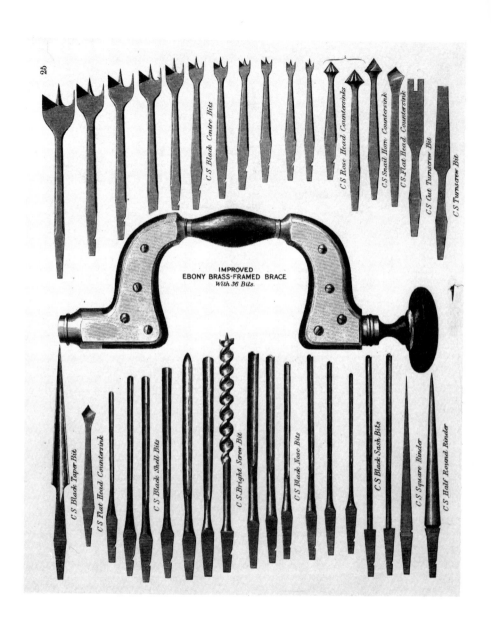

A brass-framed ebony brace of the type sold by a number of Sheffield toolmakers in the second half of the nineteenth century. Some models had a ring of ivory let into the head. Although these braces were heavier, and much costlier, than ordinary braces, without having any mechanical advantages, they were evidently popular as large numbers were sold and often engraved with their owners' names. Thirty-six bits are also shown.

22

Some Japanese tools (axe, adze, saws and hammers) in a print by Hokusai, one of several great artists who have evidently been attracted by the shapes of tools — others being Durer, Champaigne and Georges de la Tour.

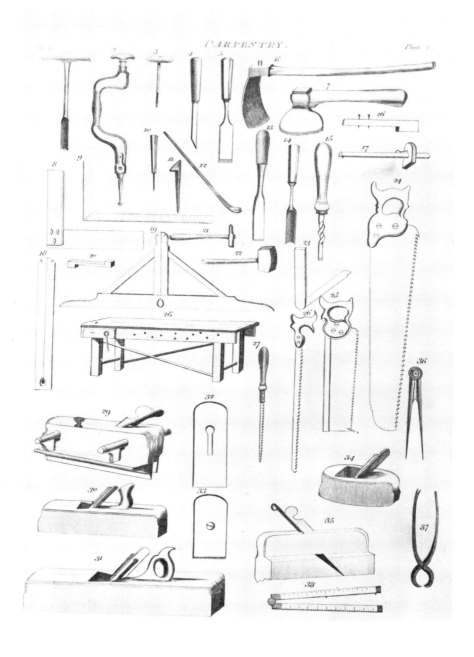

Plate illustrating carpentry tools from Thomas Martin's 'New Circle of the Mechanical Arts', 1819.

The tools of a cooper. Note how the side axe (top row, second from the left) and the adze (just above the brace, at the right of the second row) differ from similar tools used by the wheelwright (see page 28). Also shown is the jointer plane, the largest type of plane made, 5 feet (1.5m) or more in length. It is used, upside down, by pushing the staves over it so that the shavings drop out underneath.

SPECIALIST WOODWORKING TRADES

Wherever a community was large enough to support a number of woodworking tradesmen specialisations developed. In each village there would usually be a wheelwright, since the continuance of the agricultural economy depended on his skills not only to keep the carts and wagons on their wheels but also to maintain ploughs, ladders, feeding troughs and all the other implements necessary to the farm. In a small village the wheelwright was also the joiner, builder, coffin maker and other things besides. His tool kit was relatively simple although he followed so many trades. His work for each trade was satisfactory to the eye as well as to its purpose. It could hardly be otherwise since its basis was the ability to make that most perfectly func-

tional and beautiful object, the wooden wheel.

The first specialist in a rural area would be the cooper. His responsibility was the construction and maintenance of every sort of stave-built wooden container, from kegs to barrels, from buckets to washtubs. His tool kit could be reduced to a one-man load and he was therefore able to walk from village to village. There is no better way to see what can be done by hand and eye alone than to watch one of the few remaining coopers shaping staves with his side axe.

The specialist carpenter had an even simpler tool kit but, at least in areas where buildings were mainly of timber-frame construction, he was a designer and the director of a building team which could

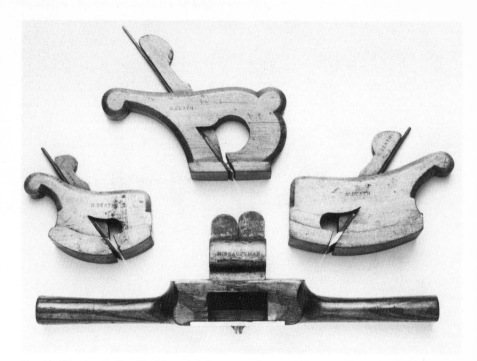

Coachbuilders' tools. Coachbuilders used the same tools as any other joiner but, in addition, they used characteristically 'tailed' planes (often home-made) and a range of routers which could be worked either right or left handed according to the direction of the grain. These three tailed planes and the moulding router came from the same kit, which had belonged to two generations of craftsmen by the name of Death and to a Mr Beautyman.

undertake to put up cottages, barns or farmhouses.

The coachbuilder and the cabinet maker were town tradesmen. Their work called for precision and a high finish. For their purposes the most elaborate tool kits were evolved. In the heyday of the cabinet-making trade — through the eighteenth century up to about 1830 — apprentices used to make magnificent chests to contain the tools and to demonstrate their own skill.

OPPOSITE: *A shipwright's tool kit. The adze is similar to the wheelwright's (page 28) except that it has a thin projecting poll for driving iron spikes below the surface of the timber being worked on. The axe was mainly used for shaping out masts and spars. The numerous iron objects in the centre are caulking chisels for stuffing oakum between the ship's boards to make it watertight. The very large chisel at the bottom, known as a slice, is the nearest thing to a thrust-axe or twybill to be used in Britain in recent years.*

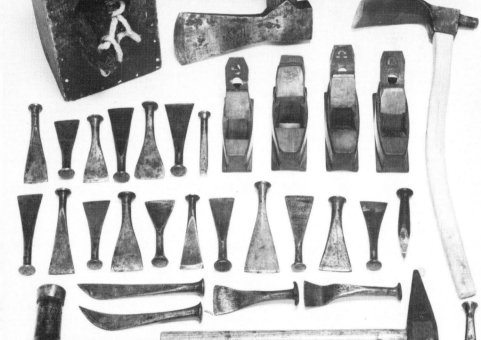

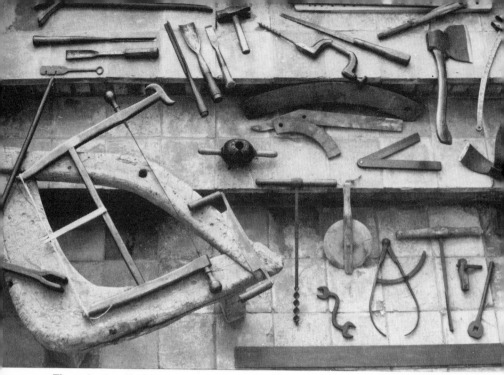

The tools of an English country wheelwright. Note particularly the side axe, the adze (upper right corner) and the large framed turning saw for cutting out wheel felloes and other curved parts.

OPPOSITE: *By the second half of the eighteenth century the most elaborate tool kits imaginable had been developed for English cabinet makers and specialist joiners. It was natural therefore that the workmen should establish a tradition of making huge and elaborately fitted tool chests. This one measures nearly 3½ feet (1060 mm) by 2½ feet (760 mm) and stands 2¼ feet (680 mm) high. It has fourteen separate drawers and compartments. Some of the tools it contained are shown, but there would also have been between fifty and one hundred moulding planes in the bottom compartment at the back of the chest.*

FURTHER READING

Bailey, Jocelyn. *Country Wheelwright.* Batsford, 1979.
Goodman, W. L. *British Planemakers from 1700.* 1978.
Goodman, W. L. *The History of Woodworking Tools.* 1964.
Kilby, K. *The Cooper and his Trade.* John Baker, 1971.
Kilby, K. *The Village Cooper* (Shire Album 28). Shire Publications Ltd, 1977.
Mercer, Henry C. *Ancient Carpenters' Tools.* 1929.
Proudfoot, Christopher, and Walker, Philip. *Woodworking Tools.* Phaidon, 1984.
Roberts, Kenneth D. *Wooden Planes in Nineteenth-Century America.* 1978.
Salaman, R. A. *Dictionary of Tools Used in the Woodworking Trades.* 1975.
Catalogues of Alex Mathieson, Thomas Norris, Stewart Spiers, Edward Preston and other
  toolmakers, reprinted by the Ken Roberts Publishing Co.
(These books, including those published in the USA, can be obtained from Roy Arnold, 77 High
Street, Needham Market, Suffolk, UK, or from other booksellers.)

PLACES TO VISIT

Some tools, including complete reconstructed workshops, can be seen in many local and
open-air museums in Britain. Collections of tools may be seen at:

GREAT BRITAIN
Bygones at Holkham, Holkham Park, Wells next the Sea, Norfolk. Telephone: Fakenham (0328)
  710806.
Clitheroe Castle Museum, Castle Hill, Clitheroe, Lancashire. Telephone: Clitheroe (0200) 24635.
The Commandery, Sidbury, Worcester WR1 2HU. Telephone: Worcester (0905) 355071.
Elvaston Working Estate Museum, Elvaston Castle, Elvaston, Derby DE7 3EP. Telephone: Derby
  (0332) 73799.
The Mead Mill Collection, Mead Mill, Mill Lane, Romsey, Hampshire SO5 8EQ. Telephone:
  Romsey (0703) 513444.
Old House Museum, Cunningham Place, Bakewell, Derbyshire DE4 1DD.
St Albans City Museum, Hatfield Road, St Albans, Hertfordshire AL1 3RR. Telephone: St Albans
  (0727) 56679.
The Science Museum, Exhibition Road, South Kensington, London SW7 2DD. Telephone: 01-589
  3456.
Towneley Hall Art Gallery and Museums, Burnley, Lancashire BB11 3RQ. Telephone: Burnley
  (0282) 24213.

OTHER COUNTRIES
Deutsches Werkzeug Museum (German Tool Museum), Hasten, Cleffstrasse 2-6, 5630 Remscheid,
  Nordrhein-Westfalen, Federal Republic of Germany.
Maison de l'Outil (Tool Museum), Hotel Mauroy, Rue de la Trinite, 10000 Troyes, France. The
  most spectacularly beautiful tool museum of all.
Mercer Museum of the Bucks County Historical Society, Pine and Ashland Streets, Doylestown,
  Pennsylvania 18901, USA.
Shelburne Museum, Route 7, Shelburne, Vermont 05482, USA.

THE TOOL AND TRADES HISTORY SOCIETY.
  Winston Grange, Stowmarket, Suffolk IP14 6LE. Founded in 1983, the TATHS exists to further
knowledge and understanding of hand tools, of their use and of the trades and craftsmen that used
them. Members receive a regular newsletter and the Journal, which contains articles and book
reviews.

OPPOSITE: *Photograph of an exceptionally fine tool chest measuring 3½ feet (1060 mm) by 2½ feet
(760 mm). It has numerous drawers and compartments and a remarkable parquetry lid and was
probably made around 1800.*

He Preached in Egipt, Africa and Britain, and at length was Crucified

The large sword-type saw designed to cut on the push stroke, shown in an engraving from a bible dated 1692, by which date it would already have appeared antiquated.